BEASTS AND THE BATTLEFIELD

BEASTS ON THE BATTLEFIELD

ANIMALS IN COMBAT

Charles C. Hofer

CAPSTONE PRESS
a capstone imprint

Captivate is published by Capstone Press, an imprint of Capstone.
1710 Roe Crest Drive, North Mankato, Minnesota 56003
www.capstonepub.com

Copyright © 2020 by Capstone. All rights reserved. No part of this publication may be reproduced in whole or in part, or stored in a retrieval system, or transmitted in any form or by any means, electronic, mechanical, photocopying, recording, or otherwise, without written permission of the publisher

Library of Congress Cataloging-in-Publication Data can be found on the Library of Congress website.
ISBN: 978-1-5435-9023-4 (hardcover)
ISBN: 978-1-4966-6593-5 (paperback)
ISBN: 978-1-5435-9028-9 (ebook PDF)

Summary: Describes various ways military forces have used animals on the front lines, and discusses notable animals and their achievements during different wars.

Editorial Credits
Aaron Sautter, editor; Kyle Grenz, designer; Morgan Walters, media researcher; Katy LaVigne, production specialist

Image Credits
Alamy: 615 collection, 21, DOD Photo, 20, PJF Military Collection, 23, Science History Images, 13, The Protected Art Archive, 5, Trinity Mirror/Mirrorpix, 15; Associated Press: Sammlung Sauer/picture-alliance/dpa, borom 26; Getty Images: Hulton Archive, 17, PAUL J. RICHARDS, 19; iStockphoto: Grafissimo, 6; Newscom: AiWire, 16, akg-images, 9, 10, Everett Collection, 25, Mirrorpix, 18, Olivier Douliery/MCT, 28, staff Mirrorpix, 11; Shutterstock: al_papito, 7, Artistdesign29, design element throughout, DFLC Prints, bottom 14, Eric Isselee, middle right 14, top 26, Janusz Baczynski, 27, Neirfy, 22, Nikolai Tsvetkov, 24, Omelchenko, design element throughout, PRESSLAB, 29, Rosa Jay, top left 14, Sammy33, 8, SasinTipchai, (elephant) Cover, Tereshchenko Dmitry, (knight) Cover, yggdrasill, 12

All internet sites appearing in back matter were available and accurate when this book was sent to press.

Printed and bound in the United States of America.
PA99

Table of Contents

A War Hero on Four Legs 4

Charging into Battle 6

Armies on the Move 12

Super Animal Senses 18

Four-Legged Friends 24

    Glossary 30

    Read More 31

    Internet Sites 31

    Index 32

Words in **bold** are in the glossary.

A War Hero on Four Legs

It was a cold day in February 1918. The American soldiers were asleep when Stubby started barking. The tiny dog sensed danger. A cloud of poison gas was headed their way. The soldiers stumbled out of bed thanks to Stubby's barks. The group of soldiers—and one brave dog—moved to safety. Stubby saved the day!

This wasn't Stubby's only heroic act during World War I (1914–1918). Stubby helped search for missing soldiers. He comforted the wounded. He even tackled an enemy soldier! After the war, Stubby became a national hero in the United States.

Animals have played many roles on the battlefield. Many have helped move armies across mountains. Some have carried secret messages. Even today, animals act as guards, find bombs, and rescue lost soldiers.

Fact
Stubby saw action in 17 battles during World War I. He earned several medals for his acts of bravery. Stubby was even given the military rank of seargent!

Charging into Battle

The War Horse

Throughout history, horses have been very important animals. Humans first tamed horses about 3500 BC. Armies soon used horses around the world.

In Ancient Egypt, horses pulled **chariots**. The speedy animals helped Egypt's soldiers strike quickly in battle. By the year AD 1200, Mongolian ruler Genghis Khan's army mastered war on horseback. By riding horses, his warriors could move swiftly against their enemies. Horses helped Khan to quickly conquer central Asia.

Horses were also prized by knights in **medieval** Europe. Armored knights on horseback were fierce warriors. They could easily defeat enemies on the ground. Horses were later brought to North America. Spanish armies used them to quickly take over parts of Mexico.

An Egyptian chariot pulled by horses

Fact

Cavalries are armed forces on horseback. They have been used throughout history. Cavalries still play minor roles on battlefields today. Some U.S. soldiers ride horses to fight in Afghanistan's rugged mountains.

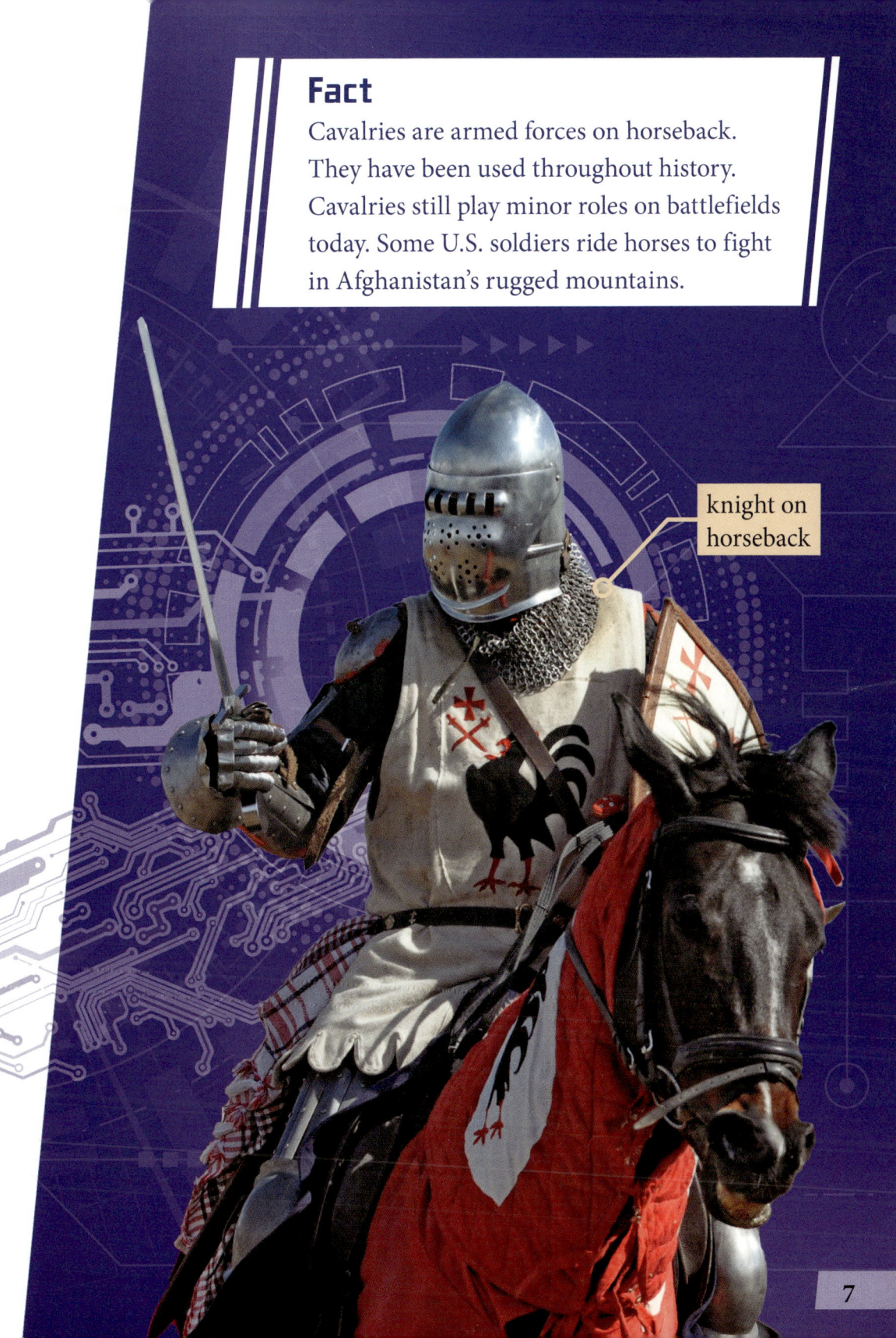

knight on horseback

Giants of the Battlefield

War elephants were important in the ancient world. The sight of these mighty beasts struck fear into enemies. Soldiers rode in battle towers on the elephants' backs. These powerful animals could easily trample enemy soldiers.

Soldiers in battle tower

Armor helped protect the elephant.

Hannibal's war elephants at the Battle of Zama in 202 BC

Carthage was an ancient empire led by Hannibal Barca. He wanted to attack the empire of Rome. At the time, Rome had the strongest army in the world. Rome was also protected by the Alps mountains. In 218 BC, Hannibal led his army and nearly 40 war elephants across the Alps. Hannibal failed in the end. But his elephants became legendary.

Fact
The Romans had a creative defense against war elephants. The big beasts are terrified of pigs. The Romans released squealing pigs onto the battlefield. It caused the elephants to run in fear.

Dogs of War

People tamed dogs more than 30,000 years ago. They were valuable hunting companions. Dogs later showed their worth in battle too.

Ancient armies often used dogs in war. Some dogs wore metal armor and spiked collars. They followed commands to attack enemies. In the 1500s, dogs helped Spanish explorers take over Mexico and Central America. They trained dogs to attack the native people.

Fact
Dogs were useful in World War I. Soldiers placed messages in containers on dogs' backs. The speedy dogs then delivered the messages across battlefields. They also helped find wounded soldiers.

message container

Soldiers train a K-9 for combat in World War II.

Dogs have amazing senses of hearing and smell. During World War II (1939–1945), the U.S. Army trained more than 10,000 guard dogs. They alerted soldiers about nearby enemies. This war dog program became known as the K-9 **Corps**.

Armies on the Move

In the Desert

Animals often help armies go where vehicles cannot. They help move troops and supplies across difficult **terrain**.

Camels can carry up to 400 pounds (181 kilograms). They can also go for a long time without water. Camels often help armies travel across hot, dry deserts.

A camel train carries heavy gear.

The Imperial Camel Corps was created in World War I. The corps helped British officer T.E. Lawrence during the war. Riding on camels, he led Arab forces into battle in North Africa.

T.E. Lawrence

Fact
The adventures of T.E. Lawrence are shown in the film *Lawrence of Arabia*.

Military Mules

A mule is the offspring of a male donkey and a female horse. These animals are smart and have **endurance**. They often make perfect pack animals.

The ancient Egyptians often used mules to pull carts and chariots. Later, Hannibal used mules to carry gear for his army. More than 1 million mules were used in the U.S. Civil War (1861–1865). They worked well in the South's swampy battlefields.

Fact
In 1899 the mule became the official **mascot** of the U.S. Army. Mules are rugged, tough, and dependable. They are the perfect symbol for American soldiers.

Mules carrying supplies in World War II.

In World War I, mule teams often pulled wagons full of equipment. Mules were also useful in World War II. They helped move armies through the jungles of Southeast Asia. Some armies still use mules today to move supplies in rough war zones.

Horses in the Great War

During World War I, tanks and cannons ruled the battlefield. Soldiers on horseback couldn't defeat these weapons. But armed forces found new uses for horses in battle.

During the war, roads were often destroyed. Some were so muddy that vehicles couldn't pass through. But this didn't stop horses. They could go where vehicles could not. Horses helped move **ammunition**, food, and equipment.

World War I was difficult for soldiers. But it was even worse for horses. The British army had 1 million horses in the war. However, only about 62,000 survived.

Horses were useful for moving equipment to areas where vehicles could not go.

Fact

Horses sometimes wore gas masks during World War I. The masks helped horses survive poison gas attacks.

soldier gas mask

horse gas masks

Super Animal Senses

Homing Pigeons

Animals with special senses often help in wartime. Homing pigeons can find their way home, even from far away. They have long been used to send messages. They can quickly deliver information over great distances.

In World War I, communicating with radios was still new. Radios didn't always work well. But pigeons were dependable. The birds delivered notes and maps to soldiers in different locations.

Soldiers attach a message to a pigeon in World War II.

Sometimes pigeons carried small automatic cameras. The cameras took battlefield photos from the air. The photos showed enemy locations.

Cher Ami, War Hero

In October 1918, some U.S. troops were trapped. They were stuck behind enemy lines in France. American gunfire exploded around them. The soldiers sent a pigeon named Cher Ami back with a message. The bird was badly wounded during the flight. But he arrived with the message. "For heaven's sake, stop it!" the note said. U.S. forces quickly changed the direction of their fire. The move saved many U.S. lives. And it was thanks to one brave little bird.

Model of Cher Ami with a small camera used in World War I

Soldiers work with dogs and metal detectors to find hidden bombs.

Bomb-Sniffing Dogs

Dogs have had many jobs on the battlefield. They've been trained as attack animals and guards. They've helped deliver messages. And they've helped find wounded soldiers.

Today many dogs help by using their super sniffers. A dog's sense of smell is 40 times stronger than a human's! This makes dogs natural bomb detectors.

Bomb-sniffing dogs are very useful on today's battlefields. **Terrorism** threatens many places around the world. Enemies often hide bombs in markets or airports. Bomb-sniffing dogs are trained to find these explosives.

Fact
U.S. forces use just a few breeds of dogs. These include shepherds and retrievers. They are smart, athletic, and easy to train.

A bomb-sniffing dog checks cars in Baghdad, Iraq.

Underwater Detectives

Some odd soldiers have important jobs today. Dolphins have a special ability called **echolocation**. It helps them find and catch food. Trained dolphins use it to find underwater mines.

The U.S. Navy began training dolphins in the 1960s. They were taught to find mines and other objects at sea. Dolphins helped keep ships safe during the Vietnam War (1954–1975.)

Fact
Dolphins work with teams of human helpers. The teams include handlers, veterinarians, and trainers.

U.S. forces still work with dolphins today. The animals use their senses to find underwater mines. If they find anything, they swim back to warn their human trainers. The mines can then be safely destroyed.

Four-Legged Friends

Search and Rescue Dogs

Dogs can do more than sniff out bombs. They can find missing people too. Wars in cities and towns can become disaster zones. Powerful weapons can destroy buildings and crumple vehicles. People can get trapped inside. Every second counts when trying to find survivors.

Thankfully, dogs can use their sense of smell to find missing people. Search and rescue (SAR) dogs are trained to focus on the smell of humans. They can quickly scramble over or under objects that slow down humans. For trapped survivors, this can mean the difference between life and death.

search and rescue dog

Fact
On September 11, 2001, terrorists crashed planes into large buildings in New York City and Washington, D.C. The attacks killed thousands of people. Nearly 300 SAR dogs worked to help find survivors in the rubble.

Mousers

Food is very important for soldiers in war. But food sometimes attracts pests like mice and rats. These hungry rodents can ruin food and spread disease. It's been a problem for armies throughout history. Luckily, nature provided a solution—the ordinary house cat.

Rats were a big problem in the trenches during World War I.

Much of World War I was fought from trenches. Troops often stayed in them for weeks at a time. Rats and mice were serious problems. They often spread disease. To fight back, militaries turned to cats. Nearly 500,000 cats were brought in to fight the pests. The cats also brought comfort to soldiers fighting on the front lines.

Wojtek the War Bear

During World War II, Polish soldiers stumbled across a baby bear. They adopted it and named it Wojtek (VOY-tek). The little cub soon grew into a huge brown bear. The soldiers loved him. But the Polish army didn't allow pets. So the soldiers gave Wojtek an army rank and put him to work. The bear helped carry heavy supplies and ammunition. After the war, Wojtek was honored as a national hero. He lived out his days at a zoo in Scotland.

A monument to Wojtek and a soldier in Edinburgh, Scotland

Faithful Friends

Today animals play another important role for soldiers. Dogs, cats, and horses are often paired with **veterans** returning home. These four-legged friends help soldiers adjust to life after war.

Therapy dogs are trained to be loyal friends. Service dogs help soldiers who may have been injured. Cats often provide comfort too. Other veterans enjoy horses. Riding and caring for horses can help soldiers return to a normal life.

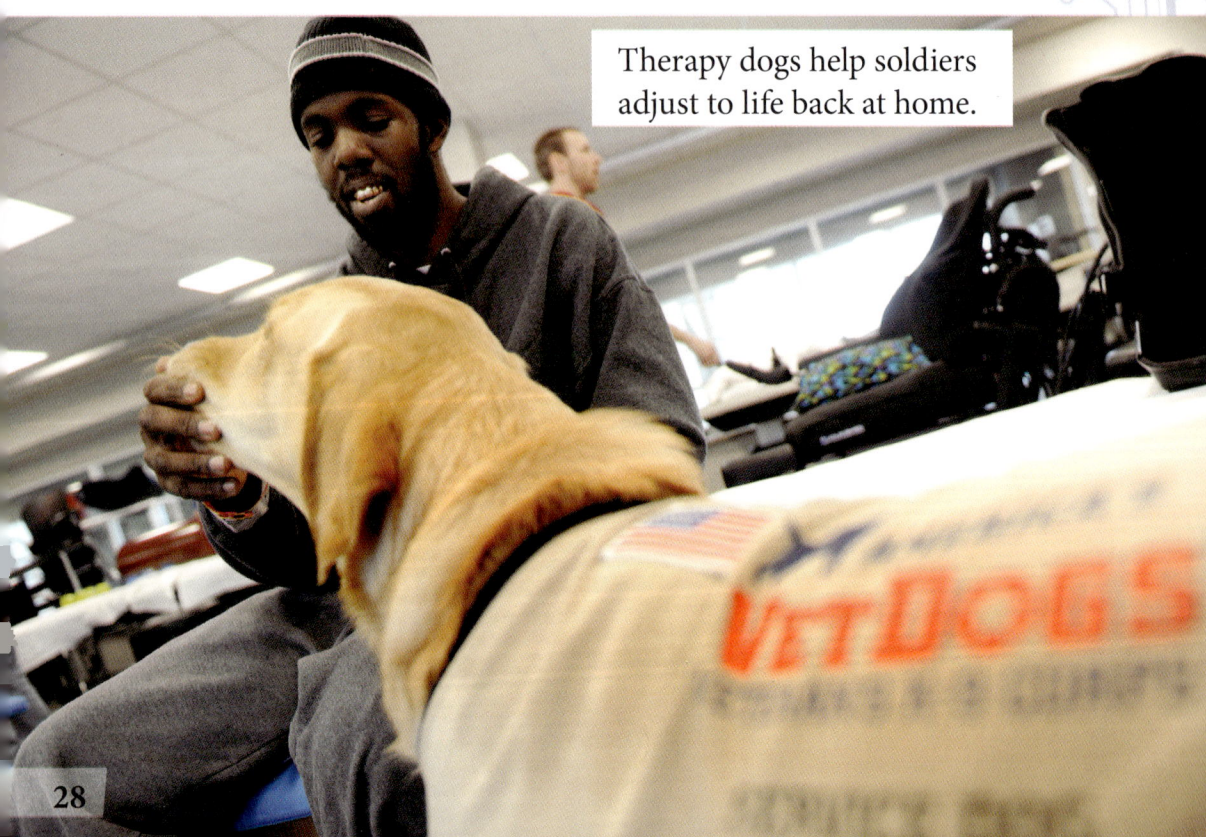

Therapy dogs help soldiers adjust to life back at home.

Animals of all shapes and sizes have long helped on the battlefield. They've carried supplies and rescued lost soldiers. They've found bombs and delivered messages. But most importantly, they are faithful friends for soldiers fighting a long way from home.

Glossary

ammunition (am-yuh-NI-shuhn)—bullets and other objects fired from weapons

chariot (CHAYR-ee-uht)—a light, two-wheeled cart pulled by horses

corps (KOR)—a military group that works together

echolocation (eh-koh-loh-KAY-shuhn)—the process of using sounds and echoes to locate objects

endurance (en-DUHR-uhnts)—the ability to keep doing an activity for long periods of time

mascot (MASS-kot)—a person, animal, or thing used to represent an organization

medieval (mee-DEE-vuhl)—having to do with the period of history between AD 500 and 1450

terrain (tuh-RAYN)—the surface of the land

terrorism (TER-ur-ih-zum)—the use of violence or force to frighten or harm others

therapy (THER-uh-pee)—treatment for illness, injury, or disability

veteran (VET-ur-uhn)—someone who served in the armed forces

Read More

Blevins, Wiley. *Military Animals.* South Egremont, MA: Red Chair Press, 2018.

Burling, Alexis. *Animals in the Military.* New York: Enslow, 2019.

McCormick, Patricia. *Sergeant Reckless: The True Story of the Little Horse Who Became a Hero.* New York: Balzer + Bray, 2017.

Internet Sites

9 Famous Animals from the First and Second World Wars
https://www.iwm.org.uk/history/9-famous-animals-from-the-first-and-second-world-wars

12 Ways Animals Have Helped the War Effort
https://www.iwm.org.uk/history/12-ways-animals-have-helped-the-war-effort

U.S. War Dogs Association, Inc.
http://www.uswardogs.org

War Animals from Horses to Glowworms
https://www.history.com/news/war-animals-from-horses-to-glowworms-7-incredible-facts

Index

animal duties
    attacking enemies, 8, 10, 20
    carrying cameras, 19
    carrying gear, 12, 14–15, 16, 29
    delivering messages, 4, 10, 18, 19, 20, 29
    finding bombs, 4, 20–21, 22–23, 24, 29
    moving armies, 4, 12, 15, 16
    providing therapy, 28
    pulling chariots and wagons, 6, 14, 15
    rescuing people, 4, 10, 20, 24, 25, 29

Barca, Hannibal, 9, 14

camels, 12–13
    Imperial Camel Corps, 13
cats, 26–27, 28
Cher Ami, 19

dogs, 10–11, 20–21, 28
    dog breeds, 21
    K-9 Corps, 11
    search and rescue (SAR) dogs, 24, 25
    Stubby the dog, 4, 5
dolphins, 22–23

elephants, 8–9

gas masks, 17

homing pigeons, 18–19
horses, 6, 14, 16, 17, 28
    armored knights, 6
    cavalries, 7

Khan, Genghis, 6

Lawrence, T.E., 13

mules, 14–15

pigs, 9

U.S. Civil War, 14

Vietnam War, 22

Wojtek the bear, 27
World War I, 4, 5, 10, 13, 15, 16, 17, 18, 27
World War II, 11, 15, 27